Modelling Figures

Upright Animals.

Modelling figures in clay. Volume2.

Upright Animals.

Introduction.

This is the second volume in our 'Clay Modelling Series.

The animals contained in the book were developed over the years and have been used to introduce basic clay modelling skills in school children of all ages. The figures are built up from simple shapes to which the students can relate.

Each project is demonstrated step by step as you work through the text, this is the technique we developed and found most effective over the years, and the objective of each step of the project is shown in the still photos. The step by step approach allows teachers to control the pace of the exercise, helping slower pupils at each stage and handing out the next piece of clay when **all** the pupils are ready.

The most important sheet in each project is the **'Worksheet'** which contains the weight of clay and the templates required to ensure the correct proportions of the models.

Each project has an element of decision making and measurement built into the worksheet with self expression encouraged in the decoration and design details applied to each model which becomes an individual creation.

Used regularly the projects will turn Teachers and Classroom Assistants into experienced modellers in clay. Repeated exposure to the techniques will encourage school staff to design and expand in-house projects. The keys are the weights, dimensions, and shapes. See **'Thirty Steps to Clay Modelling'** for further information which outlines all the basic skills needed for successful clay modelling projects.

Preparation.

The Worksheet should be made available to each work group to allow them access to the templates, we have found that one sheet to four children is a good balance.

As the sheet can come into contact with wet clay it is recommended that the master is copied and each sheet is sleeved or laminated to avoid clay smudges. Once the sheets are covered they can be kept for repeated sessions and become a school resource.

When we worked with groups the clay was prepared prior to the session.

Preparation consisted of weighing out the pieces and sealing clay for a specific purpose in a plastic bag to keep it moist.

Enjoy Your Clay Modelling.

Clay Modelling Tools.

All the tools can be bought in craft or hobby shops or you can produce cheap alternatives which are just as good and in some cases better and more suitable for use in schools.

Modelling tools shown are the simple tools needed for sculpting small models, most thumb pots and most coil pots.

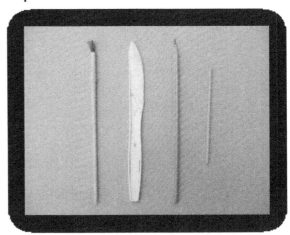

The paint brush is chosen for its stiff bristles which allow you to rough up the clay to help with cross hatching or obviate the need for cross hatching in some circumstances.

Plastic knives with the serrated edges trimmed using scissors and sharpened on sand paper are a cheap alternative to a potter's fettling knife and more suitable for use by young children. They are used primarily for cutting lengths of clay but can be used as a spatula to smooth joints between pieces of clay.

Pencils or pointed sticks, shown in the picture, are used for adding details such as eyes or hair to models or drawing patterns and designs on pots of all descriptions. The pointed stick shown was made from 3mm thick skewers used in cooking Kebabs. Cut the skewer to the length you need, I got three from one skewer, sharpen one end and round off the other end using sand paper.

The work surface shown is made from 4mm thick, three ply or MDF sheet and is 20cm x30cm.

These tools represent a one off purchase as a central resource for a school to be used by any class as required.

B&M Potterycrafts.
Modelling with clay. Volume 2.

Upright Animals.

1. Upright Dog.

2. Upright Duck.

3. Upright Hedgehog.

4. Upright Mouse.

5. Upright Pig.

6. Upright Rabbit.

B & M Potterycrafts.

Modelling Figures in Clay.

Upright Animals.

Dog.Westie.

1. Upright Dog. 9

Roll a ball. 9

Make an egg shape. 9

Head to body. 9

Make and fit the feet and arms. 10

Make and fit the tail. 11

Make and fit muzzle and ears. 12

Eyes nose and mouth. 12

Worksheet. Upright Dog. Westie. 13

1. Upright Dog.

Roll a ball.

Roll the clay between the palms of your hands, exerting sufficient force to remove any lumps or bumps. Don't be tempted to take the easy route to smooth the clay by rolling it on the wooden work surface as this removes moisture from the clay and could make it too hard for modelling. Any creases or cracks can be smoothed using the fingers.

Continue to roll the clay until the surface is smooth and the clay is the desired shape ie a ball shape.

Make an egg shape.

Take the clay ball between the palms of your hands and roll it into an egg shape. Roll the clay backwards and forwards across your palms exerting sufficient pressure to form the egg shape. The best way is to roll the clay a few times, check the shape then roll it a bit more, keep rolling and checking until you get the shape that you need. Complete the shape by rounding off the ends of the egg with your fingers.

Head to body.

Start by rolling the clay into a smooth ball to form the head and stand the body on one end .To attach the head to the body we need to make **crosshatch** marks and create **slip.** With the point of the plastic knife score **'#'** on the top of the body and on the head where it is to be joined to the body. Dip the brush in water and firmly rub the brush and water across the '#' marks, the area will turn white and this material is **slip.** Finally **press** the head and body firmly together.

The creation of **slip** is an important part of joining together two pieces of clay. The water from the brush is rubbed firmly into the clay surface until it turns light grey

Crosshatching is one of the keys to joining two pieces of clay. It consists of the scoring the pieces in the areas to be joined. Use the point of the knife to mark clay.

The use of **pressure** is essential in successfully joining two pieces of clay when used in conjunction with crosshatching and slip.

Make and fit the feet and arms.

Roll the clay into a smooth ball and then roll it backwards and forwards to form a jellybean shape to the length shown on the worksheet, cut this in half to make the feet. Use the brush and water to form slip in two patches where the feet are to fit, make slip on the feet where they have been cut and press the feet into place. No need to crosshatch as firm pressure will attach the feet and arms.

Roll the clay into a sausage to the length shown in the worksheet, cut the sausage in half to make two arms.

Create slip on the body where the arms are to fit and on the arm where it will touch the body. Press the arms firmly into place and the smooth the tops to form them to the body as shoulders.

Make and fit the tail.

To make the tail the clay must first be rolled into a ball. Roll one edge of the ball across the palm of one hand using one finger, this method of rolling will produce a short cone shape, when the cone is the required length and shape flatten the thick end on the work surface.

Create slip on the flattened end of the tail and also on the dog where the tail will fit, press the tail firmly into place.

Make and fit muzzle and ears.

The muzzle is made by rolling the clay between the fingers and thumbs of both hands simultaneously this creates a double cone shape. Fold the double cone in the centre and apply slip to one side of the clay and on the head and stick the muzzle onto the head.

Make a double cone as we did with the muzzle and cut it in half to form two ears. Apply slip to the head and to each ear and press the ears into place.

Eyes nose and mouth.

Roll a small piece of clay and attach it to the tip of the muzzle with slip.

The mouth is made by pushing the point of the wooden stick through the gap in the muzzle and the eyes are made with the point of the stick.

Push the point of the knife into the paws to make the claws as shown on the picture.

B & M Potterycrafts.

Worksheet. Upright Dog. Westie.

Clay.

Body.   80grams.

Head.   15grams.

Arms.   7grams.

Tail.   7grams.

Feet.   4grams.

Ears.   2grams.

Muzzle.   2 grams.

Scale.   5 cms.

B & M Potterycrafts.

Modelling Figures in Clay.

Upright Animals.

Duck.

Contents

2. Upright Duck. 17

    Roll a ball. 17

    Make an egg shape. 17

    Head to body. 18

    Make and fit the feet and wings. 18

    Make and fit the tail. 19

    Make and fit the beak 20

    Eyes and feathers. 20

    Worksheet. Upright Duck. 21

2. Upright Duck.

Roll a ball.

Roll the clay between the palms of your hands, exerting sufficient force to remove any lumps or bumps. Don't be tempted to take the easy route to smooth the clay by rolling it on the wooden work surface as this removes moisture from the clay and could make it too hard for modelling. Any creases or cracks can be smoothed using the fingers.

Continue to roll the clay until the surface is smooth and the clay is the desired shape i.e. a ball shape.

Make an egg shape.

Take the clay ball between the palms of your hands and roll it into an egg shape. Roll the clay backwards and forwards across your palms exerting sufficient pressure to form the egg shape. The best way is to roll the clay a few times, check the shape then roll it a bit more, keep rolling and checking until you get the shape that you need. Complete the shape by rounding off the ends of the egg with your fingers.

Head to body.

Start by rolling the clay into a smooth ball and stand the body on one end .To attach the head to the body we need to make **crosshatch** marks and create **slip.** With the point of the plastic knife score **'#'** on the top of the body and on the head where it is to be joined to the body. Dip the brush in water and firmly rub the brush and water across the '#' marks, the area will turn white and this material is **slip.** Finally **press** the head and body firmly together.

The creation of **slip** is an important part of joining together two pieces of clay. The water from the brush is rubbed firmly into the clay surface until it turns light grey

Crosshatching is one of the keys to joining two pieces of clay. It consists of the scoring the pieces in the areas to be joined. Use the point of the knife to mark clay.

The use of **pressure** is essential in successfully joining two pieces of clay when used in conjunction with crosshatching and slip.

Make and fit the feet and wings.

Roll the clay into a smooth ball and then roll it backwards and forwards to form a jellybean shape to the length shown on the worksheet, cut this in half to make the feet. Use the brush and water to form slip in two patches where the feet are to fit, make slip on the feet where they have been cut and press the feet into place. Ducks have flat feet so slightly squash the feet to flatten them a little.

Roll the clay into a ball and in the palms of your hands squash the ball to form a disc the diameter shown in the worksheet. Cut the disc in half to make two wings. Create slip on the

body where the wings are to fit and on the wing where it will touch the body. Press the wings firmly into place and smooth the tops to form them to the body.

Make and fit the tail.

To make the tail the clay must first be rolled into a ball. Roll one edge of the ball across the palm of one hand using one finger this method of rolling will produce a short cone shape, when the cone is the required length flatten the thick end on the work surface.

Create slip on the flattened end of the tail and also on the duck where the tail will fit, press the tail firmly into position. Once the tail is firmly in place press the duck's body slightly forward against the feet to make it lean forwards a little.

Make and fit the beak

The first job is to make a slot with the handle of the knife, the slot is across the front of the head as shown in the picture.

Start the beak by rolling the clay into a ball and then into a jellybean, cut the jellybean in half and roll the two pieces into two balls. Squash these balls slightly with the thumb of one hand on the palm of the other hand, to form the top and bottom parts of the beak. With the brush and water create slip in the slot by rubbing the brush firmly across the slot. Make slip on one edge of the lower part of the beak and press it into the slot sloping downwards as shown on the picture. Repeat this with the upper part of the beak but this time the beak slopes upwards.

Eyes and feathers.

on

Use the point of the wooden stick to make two holes for the duck's eyes. The point is also used to draw feathers on the wings and the tail.

B & M Potterycrafts.

Worksheet. Upright Duck.

Clay.

Body.	80grams.
Head.	15grams.
Wings.	10grams.
Tail.	4grams.
Feet.	4grams.
Beak.	1 gram.
Scale.	5 cms.

B & M Potterycrafts.

Modelling Figures in Clay.

Upright Animals.

Hedgehog.

\Contents and sequence.

Upright Hedgehog...25

Roll a ball...25

Make an egg shape. 25

Make the head. 26

Attach the head to the body...26

Model head to body..27

Make and fit the arms. 27

Nose..28

Eyes and ears..28

Spikes...28

Upright Hedgehog Worksheet...29

Upright Hedgehog.

Roll a ball.

Roll the clay between the palms of your hands, exerting sufficient force to remove any lumps or bumps. Don't be tempted to take the easy route to smooth the clay by rolling it on the wooden work surface as this removes moisture from the clay and could make it too hard for modelling. Any creases or cracks can be smoothed using the fingers. Continue to roll the clay until the surface is smooth and the clay is the desired shape i.e. a ball shape.

Make an egg shape.

Take the clay ball between the palms of your hands and roll it into an egg shape. Roll the clay backwards and forwards across your palms exerting sufficient pressure to form the egg shape. The best way is to roll the clay a few times, check the shape then roll it a bit more, keep rolling and checking until you get the shape that you need. Complete the shape by rounding off the ends of the egg with your fingers.

Make the head.

To form the head roll the clay into a smooth ball then into an egg shape, then with fingers and thumb form one end of the egg shape into a point to the shape shown on the picture.

Attach the head to the body.

To attach the head to the body we need to make **crosshatch** marks and create **slip.** With the point of the plastic knife score **'#'** on the top of the body and on the head where it is to be joined to the body. Dip the brush in water and firmly rub the brush and water across the '#' marks, the area will turn white and this material is **slip.** Finally **press** the head and body firmly together.

The creation of **slip** is an important part of joining together two pieces of clay. The water from the brush is rubbed firmly into the clay surface until it turns light grey

Crosshatching is one of the keys to joining two pieces of clay. It consists of the scoring the pieces in the areas to be joined. Use the point of the knife to mark clay.

The use of **pressure** is essential in successfully joining two pieces of clay when used in conjunction with crosshatching and slip.

Model head to body.

With your finger or thumb smooth clay from the head onto the body, the modelling is from one side of the head to the other side, not under the chin.

Make and fit the feet.

Roll the clay into a smooth ball and then roll it backwards and forwards to form a jellybean shape to the length shown on the worksheet, cut this in half to make the feet. Use the brush and water to form slip in two patches where the feet are to fit, make slip on the feet where they have been cut and press the feet into place.

Make and fit the arms.

Roll the clay into a sausage to the length shown in the worksheet, cut the sausage in half to make two arms.

Create slip on the body where the arms are to fit and on the arm where it will touch the body. Press the arms firmly into place and the smooth the tops to form them to the body as shoulders.

Make the nose.

Take a small piece of clay and roll it into a ball, dip the brush in water and rub the water on the top of the pointed end of the head and on one side of the small ball press the nose firmly onto the face.

Eyes and ears.

The eyes are easily made with the pointed end of the stick, push the point into the clay in the positions shown on the worksheet.

Use the pointed end of the stick again to make curly c's to represent the ears.

Spikes.

Hold your knife like a pencil and carefully draw short lines from the head down to the tail end of the hedgehog, start between the ears and cover the back and sides of the model.

Hedgehogs don't have spikes on their stomachs so leave the front smooth.

B & M Potterycrafts.

Upright Hedgehog Worksheet.

Clay and Sequence.

Body.   80grams.

Head.   15grams.

Arms.   7grams.   7cms.

Feet.   4grams.

Nose.   Small piece.

It is important to copy
this sheet to scale.

B & M Potterycrafts.

Modelling Figures in Clay.

Upright Animals.

Mouse.

Table of Contents

Upright Mouse. 33

   Roll a ball.. 33

   Make an egg shape...................................... 33

   Head to body... 34

   Make and fit the feet and arms................... 35

   Make and fit tail.. 35

   Eyes and ears, nose and toes. 36

   Upright Mouse Worksheet. 37

Upright Mouse.

Roll a ball.

Roll the clay between the palms of your hands, exerting sufficient force to remove any lumps or bumps. Don't be tempted to take the easy route to smooth the clay by rolling it on the wooden work surface as this removes moisture from the clay and could make it too hard for modelling. Any creases or cracks can be smoothed using the fingers. Continue to roll the clay until the surface is smooth and the clay is the desired shape i.e. a ball shape.

Make an egg shape.

Take the clay ball between the palms of your hands and roll it into an egg shape. Roll the clay backwards and forwards across your palms exerting sufficient pressure to form the egg shape. The best way is to roll the clay a few times, check the shape then roll it a bit more, keep rolling and checking until you get the shape that you need. Complete the shape by rounding off the ends of the egg with your fingers.

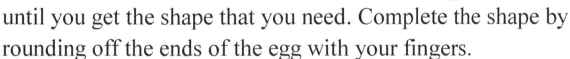

Head to body.

To form the head roll the clay into a smooth ball and then
into an egg shape, with fingers and
thumb form one end of the egg
shape into a point to the shape
shown on the picture.

To attach the head to the body we need to make **crosshatch**
marks and create **slip.** With the point of
the plastic knife score **'#'** on the top
of the body and on the head where
it is to be joined to the body. Dip the
brush in water and firmly rub the
brush and water across the '#' marks, the
area will turn white and this material is **slip.** Finally **press** the
head and body firmly together.

The creation of **slip** is an important part of joining together two pieces of clay. The water from the brush is rubbed firmly into the clay surface until it turns light grey

Crosshatching is one of the keys to joining two pieces of clay. It consists of the scoring the pieces in the areas to be joined. Use the point of the knife to mark clay.

The use of **pressure** is essential in successfully joining two pieces of clay when used in conjunction with crosshatching and slip.

Make and fit the feet and arms.

Roll the clay into a smooth ball and then roll it backwards and forwards to form a jellybean shape to the length shown on the worksheet, cut this in half to make the feet.

Use the brush and water to form slip in two patches where the feet are to fit, make slip on the feet where they have been cut and press the feet into place. No need to crosshatch as firm pressure will attach the feet and arms.

Roll the clay into a sausage to the length shown in the worksheet, cut the sausage in half to make two arms.

Create slip on the body where the arms are to fit and on the arm where it will touch the body. Press the arms firmly into place and the smooth the tops to form them to the body as shoulders.

Make and fit tail.

Roll the clay into a sausage to the length of his body as shown on the picture.

Create slip along the back of the mouse also along the length of the tail, press the tail firmly into place.

Eyes and ears, nose and toes.

With the wooden stick make two holes for the eyes.

Roll the clay into a ball, then into sausage shape. Cut the sausage in half and roll the two pieces onto small balls finally squash them slightly to form two discs for the ears.

Use the thick end of the knife to make two slots where the ears are to be fitted.

Create slip in the slots with brush and water also on the edge of each ear, press the ears firmly into the slots.

Roll a small piece of clay into a ball, make slip on the end of the face and the small ball and press the nose firmly into place.

Finally use the point of the knife to draw whiskers on the nose and press the point into the paws to make the toes.

B & M Potterycrafts.

Upright Mouse Worksheet.

Clay.

Body.   **80grams.**

Head.   **15grams.**

Arms.   **7grams.**

Tail.   **5grams**

Feet.   **4grams.**

Ears.   **2grams.**

Scale.   **5 cms.**

Modelling Figures in Clay.

Upright Animals.

Pig.

Table of Contents

Upright Pig. 41

Roll a ball. 41

Make an egg shape. 41

Head to body. 41

Make and fit the feet and arms. 42

Make and fit tail and ears. 43

Worksheet. 44

Upright Pig.

Roll a ball.

Roll the clay between the palms of your hands, exerting sufficient force to remove any lumps or bumps. Don't be tempted to take the easy route to smooth the clay by rolling it on the wooden work surface as this removes moisture from the clay and could make it too hard for modelling. Any creases or cracks can be smoothed using the fingers. Continue to roll the clay until the surface is smooth and the clay is the desired shape ie a ball shape.

Make an egg shape.

Take the clay ball between the palms of your hands and roll it into an egg shape. Roll the clay backwards and forwards across your palms exerting sufficient pressure to form the egg shape. The best way is to roll the clay a few times, check the shape then roll it a bit more, keep rolling and checking until you get the shape that you need. Complete the shape by rounding off the ends of the egg with your fingers.

Head to body.

To form the head roll the clay into a smooth ball then into an egg shape, finally with fingers and thumb form one end of the egg shape into a point to the shape shown on the picture.

To attach the head to the body we need to make **crosshatch** marks and create

41

slip. With the point of the plastic knife score **'#'** on the top of the body and on the head where it is to be joined to the body. Dip the brush in water and firmly rub the brush and water across the '#' marks, the area will turn white and this material is **slip.** Finally **press** the head and body firmly together.

Press the pointed end of the head flat with the blade of the knife to form the snout. Use the pointed stick to make two eyes and two nostrils on the snout. To complete the face use the edge of the knife to cut a slit for the mouth.

The creation of **slip** is an important part of joining together two pieces of clay. The water from the brush is rubbed firmly into the clay surface until it turns light grey

Crosshatching is one of the keys to joining two pieces of clay. It consists of the scoring the pieces in the areas to be joined. Use the point of the knife to mark clay.

The use of **pressure** is essential in successfully joining two pieces of clay when used in conjunction with crosshatching and slip.

Make and fit the feet and arms.

Roll the clay into a smooth ball and then roll it backwards and forwards to form a jellybean shape to the length shown on the worksheet, cut this in half to make the feet. Use the brush and water to form slip in two patches where the feet are to fit, make slip on the feet where they have been cut and press the feet into place.

Roll the clay into a sausage to the length shown in the worksheet, cut the sausage in half to make two arms.

Create slip on the body where the arms are to fit and on the arm where it will touch the body. Press the arms firmly into place and the smooth the tops to form them to the body as shoulders.

Make and fit tail and ears.

Roll the small piece of clay for the tail into a short sausage shape, create slip at the back of the pig and along the whole length of the tail. Press one end of the tail into the slip on the body curl the tail with finger and thumb and press the tail onto the body.

Take the clay for the ears and give it two rolls on the palms of your hands to make a jelly bean shape. Cut the jelly bean in half and roll the two pieces into two balls. Squash the balls on the palm of one

hand with the thumb of the other hand two make two flat discs to represent ears. Make slip in two patches on the head, use the picture for positioning, also make slip on the ears where they will fit to the head and press them into place.

Complete the modelling with the point of your knife to give the pig 'trotters' as shown in the picture.

B & M Potterycrafts.

Worksheet.   Upright Pig.

Clay.

Body.   80grams.

Head.   15grams.

Arms.   7grams.

Tail.   1gram.

Feet.   4grams.

Ears.   2grams.

Scale.   5 cms.

B & M Potterycrafts.

Modelling Figures in Clay.

Upright Animals.

Rabbit.

Table of Contents

Upright Rabbit. 47

Roll a ball. 47

Make an egg shape. 47

Make and fit the head. 48

Make and fit the feet and tail. 49

Make and fit the arms and ears. 49

Finishing details. 50

Worksheet. 51

Upright Rabbit.

Roll a ball.

Roll the clay between the palms of your hands, exerting sufficient force to remove any lumps or bumps. Don't be tempted to take the easy route to smooth the clay by rolling it on the wooden work surface as this removes moisture from the clay and could make it too hard for modelling. Any creases or cracks can be smoothed using the fingers. Continue to roll the clay until the surface is smooth and the clay is the desired shape ie a ball shape.

Make an egg shape.

Take the clay ball between the palms of your hands and roll it into an egg shape. Roll the clay backwards and forwards across your palms exerting sufficient pressure to form the egg shape. The best way is to roll the clay a few times, check the shape then roll it a bit more, keep rolling and checking until you get the shape that you need. Complete the shape by rounding off the ends of the egg with your fingers.

Make and fit the head.

To form the head roll the clay into a smooth ball then into an egg shape.

To attach the head to the body we need to make **crosshatch** marks and create **slip**

With the point of the plastic knife score **'#'** on the top of the body and on the head where it is to be joined to the body. Dip the brush in water and firmly rub the brush and water across the '#' marks, the area will turn white and this material is **slip.** Finally **press** the head and body firmly together.

Note.

The creation of **slip** is an important part of joining together two pieces of clay. The water from the brush is rubbed firmly into the clay surface until it turns light grey

Crosshatching is one of the keys to joining two pieces of clay. It consists of the scoring the pieces in the areas to be joined. Use the point of the knife to mark clay.

The use of **pressure** is essential in successfully joining two pieces of clay when used in conjunction with crosshatching and slip.

Make and fit the feet and tail.

Roll the clay into a smooth ball and then roll it backwards and forwards to form a jellybean shape to the length shown on the worksheet, cut this in half to make the feet. Use the brush and water to form slip in two patches where the feet are to fit, make slip on the feet where they have been cut and press the feet into place.

To make the tail simply roll a small ball, make slip on the body and on the tail and press the tail into place.

Make and fit the arms and ears.

Roll the clay into a sausage to the length shown in the worksheet, cut the sausage in half to make two arms.

Create slip on the body where the arms are to fit and on the arm where it will touch the body. Press the arms firmly into place and the smooth the tops to form them to the body as shoulders.

To form the rabbit's ears roll the clay into a sausage shape the, length is as shown on the worksheet. With the thumb slightly flatten the sausage shape and cut it in half to form two ears.

The rabbit shown is a floppy eared or lop eared rabbit and the ears are fixed with slip as shown in the picture, blend the ears into the head to complete the joint.

Finishing details.

Eyes. These are made with the pointed end of the wooden stick at each side of the rabbit's head.

Mouth. Use the sharp edge of the knife to create the mouth.

Press the edge into the end of the egg shaped head.

Claws. Use the tip of the knife pressed carefully into the paws to make the rabbit's claws as shown in the picture.

Completed Rabbit.

Worksheet.

Upright Rabbit.

Clay.

Body.   80grams.

Head.   15grams.

Arms.   8grams.

Tail.   1grams.

Feet.   4grams.

Ears.   8grams

Scale.   5 cms.

Made in the USA
Las Vegas, NV
23 March 2025

19984548R00031